Invest and Beat the Pros - Create and Manage a Successful Investment Portfolio

Best Research Supported Index Fund Strategy

Barbara A. Friedberg, MBA, MS

BarbaraFriedbergPersonalFinance.com

"In an efficient market, at any point in time, the actual price of a security will be a good estimate of its intrinsic value."

Eugene Fama, 2013 Nobel Prize winner in economics

Investing in index funds is a proven way to grow your earnings into lifelong financial security.

Fama's research surrounding efficient capital markets led to the development of the index fund, currently the most popular type of investment. You will (likely) beat 60 percent to 70 percent of active mutual fund managers investing with this index fund approach, and this Nobel Prize winning theory is easy to set up and manage.

This is not a get rich scheme, but a practical investing approach anyone can implement, follow and administer for the long haul.

Does this sound like you?

Are you worried about your financial future?

Would you like a method to set up your finances for success now, and financial security later?

Do you feel like you lack time and knowledge to properly manage your money?

Have you made money mistakes in the past?

If you answered yes to any of these questions, this investing blueprint offers a solution to your money planning concerns.

Practically, I understand that beating investment pros is great, but even more important than that is understanding **how to invest to reach your personal investment goals**.

Here's how you'll benefit and what you'll learn from this investing blueprint:

1. The index fund investing approach that helps you reach your financial goals.

2. Enough investing knowledge to create your own investment strategy and avoid making poor choices.
3. Explanations of common money terms, to increase your investing literacy.
4. The skill to determine whether you need an advisor, and what to look for if you want additional financial guidance.
5. An understanding of how you'll respond to the ups and downs in the investing markets and, more importantly, how to invest so you'll be comfortable and not racked with money worries during all economic scenarios.
6. How to narrow down the field of mutual fund and exchange traded funds (ETFs) into a manageable number.
7. A clear picture of which investments to choose with sample portfolios to guide you.
8. How to integrate your workplace retirement account with your other financial accounts.
9. A plan to maintain your investment portfolio for the long term, in minimal time, so you'll have the money you need for your financial goals, now and later.

With this book, you have in hand a blueprint for an investment approach that beats most professional active mutual fund managers. But more importantly, you'll learn to maximize your investment returns using research-based proven investing strategies.

Take a few hours to set up your investments today, in order to build wealth to spend on what's important to you later.

Barbara Friedberg, MBA, MS is a former investment portfolio manager, author of *Personal Finance; An Encyclopedia of Modern Money Management* and *How to Get Rich; Without Winning the Lottery.* Friedberg is a former university investments instructor, and publisher of BarbaraFriedbergPersonalFinance.com. Her work has been featured in *US News &World Report, Investopedia,* Yahoo! Finance, and *Investor's Business Daily.* Follow her on **Twitter** (https://twitter.com/barbfriedberg) and **Google+** (https://plus.google.com/+BarbaraFriedberg/posts).

Free Bonus Download:

Complimentary Micro book,
Barbara Friedberg Personal Finance; The Readers' Favorites
http://forms.aweber.com/form/43/1333323943.htm

Please enjoy this complimentary micro book as my gift to you.

This specially crafted micro book includes 35 pages of Barbara Friedberg Personal Finance.com Readers' Favorites articles. There is something here for everyone.

The first article, ironically discusses how trading in a newer car, just might make sense. The takeaway is that there is no one right way to handle your money. Following are creative ways to make money and a special article about how to beat the lottery.

The investing articles discuss whether bonds are a good place to invest, and if you should pay off your mortgage or invest in the stock market. Another investing piece is actually three posts in one, with questions from several of my newbie investors.

Finally, what is money worth, if your life is unfulfilled? Another article asks and attempts to answer the question "Is Money the Only Measure of Success?" Ultimately, who doesn't want a wealthy life? The micro book looks at wealth in a more global way with "58 Habits to Increase Wealth".

Please enjoy Barbara Friedberg Personal Finance; The Readers' Favorites micro book and feel free to forward this link to anyone else who might benefit from it.

Barbara Friedberg Personal Finance; The Readers' Favorites
http://forms.aweber.com/form/43/1333323943.htm

Contents

Chapter 1:
What Is the Investing Strategy That Beats the Pros?

"So investors shouldn't delude themselves about beating the market. They're just not going to do it. It's just not going to happen."

Daniel Kahneman, Nobel Laureate in Economics, 2002

As a 30 year investing veteran, portfolio manager and university investments instructor who reached her retirement goals a while ago, I want to share what I've learned about investing with you. You'll also discover what Nobel Prize winners, academicians, and many financial experts have proven works in growing your money by investing.

> ## Asset Classes Index Fund Investing Beats Professional Portfolio Mangers 70 Percent of the Time

The first day in my *Investments* class in the Penn State MBA program, the professor said, "Raise your hand if you think you can outperform the markets." My hand shot up. After all, I was a portfolio manager with a solid investing record. I was fully confident that I could outperform the markets.

Throughout the class, I delved into the research and totally revamped my investing approach based upon the data. That's right, there is evidence which defines the most successful investing approaches. Turns out, **diversification based upon asset classes in line with your risk tolerance leads to returns which outperform professional investors 60 to 70 percent of the time.**

Don't just take my opinion; in addition to Nobel Prize winner Daniel Kahneman, there are scores of well-known economists and investors who support this investing approach.

A few of the proponents of index fund investing based upon asset classes include John Bogle, the founder of Vanguard Funds, Warren Buffett, Rick Ferri, author and *Forbes* columnist, Nouriel Rubini, the economist who predicted the 2008 housing collapse and subsequent recession, Dr. William Bernstein, widely acclaimed investment researcher and author, David Swenson, Chief Investment Officer of Yale University's Endowment Fund, and countless others.

The research on asset classes is clear, 60 to 70 percent of active mutual fund managers fail to beat the indexes each year.

Why Not Invest With the 30-40 Percent of Active Managers Who Beat the Index Funds Each Year?

What about the 30 to 40 percent of professional managers who beat the indexes? Why not invest with those outperforming managers or pick stocks and beat them yourself?

Here's the problem. Even if a professional outshines the index one year, and let's say the manager is really skilled and outperforms the next year as well, over the long term it is almost impossible for anyone to consistently beat the indexes.

Mark Hulbert, in the May 10, 2013 *Wall Street Journal* article "Man vs. Machine: The Great Stock Showdown", asks us to "Consider the 51 advisers out of more than 200 on the *Hulbert Financial Digest's* list who beat the market in the decade-long period that ended April 30, 2012 (as measured by the Wilshire 5000 Total Market index, including reinvested dividends).

"Of that group, just 11—or 22 percent—have outperformed the overall market since then. That's no better than the percentage that applies to all advisers, regardless of past performance. Over the past year, on average, the group has lagged the Wilshire index by 6.2 percentage points.

In other words, going with a recent market beater doesn't increase your odds of future success."

What about George Soros or Warren Buffett? Okay, maybe there are one or two investors in the world who outperform the indexes over the long term. Ask yourself this, "Are they really that skilled or just unbelievably lucky?" And what are your odds at beating the indexes?

If you would like advice from Warren Buffett, Berkshire Hathaway, Inc., read what he said in a 1996 shareholder letter, "The best way to own common stocks is through index funds…"

INDEX FUND INVESTING PROOF: HOT OFF THE PRESS

According to 2014 Vanguard research by Philips, Kinniry, Schlanger, and Hirt in "The Case for Index-fund Investing"[1], the index fund approach continues to beat active management strategies.

The Vanguard researchers clearly explained how investing in the markets is a "zero sum" activity. In other words, when one person buys Apple stock, there must be another individual selling Apple stock shares. Continuing with the zero sum concept, when one investor outperforms, another underperforms.

Wait, that doesn't add up to a win for most index fund investors and a loss for most active fund managers. There are missing pieces to this "zero sum" example.

The missing pieces are costs and fees for buying and selling the individual securities and funds. Every mutual fund has management costs, and most buy and sell stock and ETF (exchange traded fund) trades tack on a commission.

When fees are factored into returns, the number of market beating fund managers shrinks.

When you take fees into account it's quite tough to beat market investment returns. (Market returns refer to the gains and losses by unmanaged stock and bond indexes such as the S & P 500 Index).

This recent Vanguard research set out to compare the investment returns between active and passive, index fund investing. The study looked at a variety of U.S. and international equity (stock) funds as well as fixed (bond) funds. The research excluded any funds from the study which closed during the time period studied. So only surviving funds during the entire study were examined.

The results upheld the benefit of index fund investing. **This investigation confirmed that active fund managers underperformed their specified benchmarks throughout most fund categories and time periods studied.**

For example, 68 percent of U.S. large-cap value stock funds did worse than their benchmark indices over the ten years prior to December 31, 2013.

Flip the example around and only 32 percent of active U.S. large-cap value stock fund managers beat their benchmark index returns. Similar results held true over shorter time periods as well. In this example, the index fund investing strategy beat active fund managers 68 percent of the time.

Fees matter.

Do you know the annual fee your mutual funds charge? What about how much you pay per stock or ETF trade? If not, you're missing an understanding of a potential drain on your investment returns.

More support of this index fund investing approach comes

when you compare the difference between the fees charged by unmanaged index mutual and exchange traded funds and those charged by active fund managers.

Lose just one percent annually to fees and your returns are penalized thousands of dollars over a lifetime.

Paying an additional 0.5 percent fee (when investing in an actively managed fund) to manage a $50,000 portfolio costs you $250 the first year. Repeat the $250 cost each year for 25 years and you sacrificed the potential for an extra $16,885, after 25 years (assume that $250 was invested each year and returned 6.5 percent annually).

So, in case you missed it, paying an extra half of one percent each year in fees costs you almost 17,000 dollars in potential returns over an investing lifetime. That's enough to pay for an extra year or two in retirement, when added to social security. Or you could put down 50 percent on a new car with the money saved.

Paying low fees when investing is really important over the long term.

That active mutual fund manager must be spectacular for 25 years to make up for the extra half or full percent you're paying him or her.

Take a look at the difference in fees between the average actively managed mutual fund and a low cost index or exchange traded fund.

Fee Comparison Between Actively Managed Funds Versus Index Mutual and Exchange Traded Funds				
Asset Class	Fund Type	Actively Managed Funds	Index Funds	ETFs
U.S. Stocks	Large-cap	0.80	0.11	0.14
	Mid-cap	0.97	0.18	0.25
	Small-cap	1.04	0.19	0.23
International Stocks	Developed Market	0.91	0.17	0.29
	Emerging Market	1.16	0.21	0.42
U.S. Bonds	Corporate	0.58	0.11	0.13
	Government	0.47	0.12	0.15

Source: The Vanguard Group[1]

THE DATA DOESN'T LIE

The Vanguard research was very clear. During most five year periods, an index fund approach handsomely beat an active fund strategy in all of the fund categories.

During the five years ending in 1998, the large blend index fund category, beat actively managed funds 94 percent of the time. If we examine the 5 year trailing returns for all of the categories ending in 2013, the small blend index fund category beat actively managed small cap blend funds 80 percent of the time.

The reasons the index fund approach, using asset classes, is so successful is that risk is controlled—through diversification and fees are slashed.

This approach isn't subject to the style drift problem of

many active fund managers. In other words, the active manager purports investing according to a certain style, such as a large capitalization value approach, but when that approach falls out of favor, the manager may swing towards another approach. This can cause less consistent results.

Finally, the index fund investing approach is so successful because this method keeps management fees, commissions, and taxes at rock bottom.

Are you convinced yet that asset classes investing with index funds is the way to best professional money managers? This investing approach is the closest you'll get to a consistently successful blueprint.

Next, find out the components which make up this successful portfolio management plan.

WHAT ARE ASSET CLASSES?

Here's where you get some background in the building blocks of an index fund investing approach.

Think of an asset class as a group of similar financial securities. Stock, bond, and cash are the most widely used asset classes.

In the 'stock asset class' you'll find broad stock index funds which attempt to mirror the entire U.S. stock market such as the Vanguard Total Stock Market Index Fund (VTSMX). You might also find an international stock fund in the broad stock asset class. Any type of financial security which has stocks in it would be considered a member of this group.

The 'bond or fixed asset class' includes corporate, municipal, or junk bond mutual and exchange traded funds. Or, you might find a total bond market fund such as Schwab Total Bond Market Index Fund (SWLBX) which includes a variety of types and sizes of U.S. bonds with varying maturities. (A maturity is the end date of an individual bond, when the bond holder gets the original investment returned.)

The cash asset class includes certificates of deposit and money market funds. Sometimes the cash asset class is rolled into the fixed asset class. Although recently cash offers low returns, this hasn't always been the case. Don't overlook the psychological benefit of having a cash cushion in your portfolio. That way, when investment values drop, you'll have extra cash available to pick up bargain priced stock and bond index funds.

Take a look at Kevin's asset mix. For example, in Kevin's stock asset class he owns a diversified U.S. stock index fund and a diversified international stock index fund.

His fixed asset class includes a total U.S. Bond fund. He also holds several thousands of dollars' worth of Government I bonds in his Treasurydirect.com[2] account. Seems like Kevin owns funds from both the stock and fixed asset classes.

WHAT RETURN CAN I EXPECT WITH ASSET CLASSES INDEX FUNDS INVESTING?

We use history to guide our estimates of future returns because the perfect crystal ball hasn't been invented yet. There's no proof that history will repeat, although in the 30 years I've been investing, U.S. and global businesses have grown.

As long as world economies prosper, investors can participate in their growth by purchasing stock, bond, and real estate index mutual and exchange traded funds (ETF).

When companies grow, their stock prices go up. As Warren Buffett publicly implied, it's likely that financial assets will continue to appreciate.

This chart demonstrates the average annual returns of stocks, bonds, and treasury bills from 1928 through 2013. This time period includes wars, recessions, depressions, and boom times. Answath Damodaran[3] of New York University regularly updates the historical market return data.

HISTORICAL ASSET CLASSES RETURNS 1928-2013

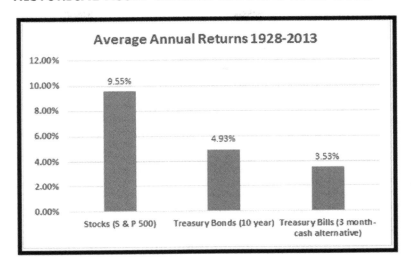

WHY STOCK RETURNS ARE USUALLY HIGHER THAN THOSE OF BONDS AND BILLS

From 1928 through 2013, the average annual return of the stock market was 9.55 percent. If you invested one hundred dollars in the stock market in 1928 and didn't touch it until 2013, that $100 would be worth $232,837 at the end of 2013.

That's quite impressive.

As you can see from the chart, stocks offered higher returns than bonds, which performed better than Treasury Bills and cash assets. If this is the case, why not invest all of your money in stocks?

During the worst years, a diversified stock portfolio could fall 10, 20, 30 percent or more. If your $10,000 investment portfolio dropped 30 percent in one year to $7,000, you'd probably be a bit upset.

Conversely, this total stock portfolio could also increase. You would be thrilled if the stock portion of your investments grew $3,333 in one year from $10,000 to $13,333 during a 30 percent return year.

Similar scenarios occurred during the last ten years.

Let's look at the returns of the recent bull market.

> In 2013, the S & P 500 returned close to 30 percent.
>
> In 2012, the S & P 500 increased 13.4 percent.
>
> In 2011, the stock market returned 2.07 percent.
>
> In 2010 the market was up 14.82 percent.

Notice that even during positive gain years, there's quite a bit of volatility in market returns.

If you want the opportunity to generate higher returns, you need to be willing to pay the price. The price for expected higher stock and bond fund returns is greater risk, or price volatility.

Before you get too excited about the possible 9 percent annual stock market returns, let's look at some down years.

> In 2008, the stock market dropped a painful 36.55 percent.
>
> In 2002, the markets were down 21.97 percent.

So you see, stocks have a long term average return close to 10 percent, but during those years there was a lot of volatility and unpredictability.

Bond prices go up and down as well, but less so than stocks. And because cash doesn't go up and down in value, it is the least risky financial asset and also offers the lowest return.

THE INVESTING STRATEGY THAT BEATS THE PROS

If history continues, and you choose a diversified portfolio of index funds in a variety of asset classes, then you can expect a return in proportion to the amounts invested in each asset class.

In other words, in a given year, if you invest 50 percent in stock index funds, and 50 percent in fixed index funds, your returns will mirror those of the index returns in direct proportion. If stocks return 12 percent and bonds return 4 percent, then your 50:50 percent asset allocation will grow 8 percent [(.50 x .12) + (.50 x .08)]. With a $10,000 investment portfolio, at the end of the year you'll have $10,800 in your account!

So, all in all, keeping investing simple with an index fund approach while avoiding overhyped promises from market 'professionals' will generally net you a market matching return. As you learned, matching the market is a more profitable path than attempting to shoot for the stars and falling short.

SUMMARY

✓ An index fund is a type of mutual or exchange traded fund which is created to track the construction of a market index, such as the Standard & Poor's 500 Index (S & P 500), or a Small-Capitalization Stock Index.

✓ Well regarded economists and Nobel Prize winners recommend investing in index funds, in accordance with your risk level.

✓ An asset class is a group of similar types of investments. The stock asset class includes individual stocks, stock mutual funds, and stock ETFs.

✓ Historically, stocks offer investors the highest returns, with bonds coming in second, and cash assets such as savings accounts and money market funds offering the lowest returns.

✓ A diversified portfolio of index funds, invested in line with one's asset allocation, has outperformed the returns of most active mutual fund portfolio managers.

Chapter 2:
Be Smart -
Before You Invest

"A goal without a plan is just a wish."

Antoine de Saint-Exupéry

As Antoine de Saint-Exupery suggests, the plan maps the drive to your goal. Conversely, no plan, no goal, no success.

Before you drop a dime into the investment markets, you need some investing background information. Just like learning to drive, you don't just get in the car and go. Before getting behind the wheel there are certain driving basics you need to understand. The same goes for investing.

INVESTING WISDOM

Why invest?

Invest today so you have money for your future wants and needs. Those future plans might include a home down payment, college for your children, and retirement.

Compare investing with keeping your money in a bank certificate of deposit or savings account. With a 1 percent savings account interest rate, your $1,000 will be worth $1,010 at the end of the year. With a 6.5 percent investment return, your $1,000 will be worth $1,065 at the end of the year. That's quite a difference between saving and investing.

How will your money grow into the future with these interest rates?

Over 30 years, with a 1 percent return, your initial $1,000 is worth $1,348. If you invest that $1,000 in a diversified portfolio of stock and bond index funds, and you receive an average annual return of 6.5 percent, then at the end of 30 years your $1,000 is worth $6,614.

That is why you invest.

Be aware that investing is only for long term goals. If you need money in five years or less, then place those funds in a short-term certificate of deposit, <u>Government I bond</u>[1], or money market mutual fund.

Here's why investing is only for long term goals. Investing offers the opportunity for higher returns, but along with those higher returns comes greater volatility. You don't want the $40,000 you need for a home down payment in three years to drop in value to $30,000 in year two, leaving you with insufficient funds for your new home down payment.

INVESTING CAUTION

Investing in the financial markets is different than putting money in a savings account.

Investments in the markets offer higher returns in exchange for greater risk. Risk means your investment value may go up and down a bit over the years. It's usual for a stock or bond mutual fund to go up in value for a few years and also to drop in value some years.

Before plunking down a large amount of money into any asset, there are several factors to consider.

Know the economic climate and the overall valuation of the S & P 500 stock market index. Do not put a large sum of money into the stock market when valuations are high.

Both individual stocks and stock market indexes have a price tag, called a <u>price earnings ratio</u>[2] (PE). The PE ratio is the current stock price divided by its earnings. Higher PE ratios equate to more expensive valuations. Lower PE ratios usually indicate undervaluation.

In February, 2014, the PE ratio for the S & P 500 index, a proxy for the U.S. stock market, was approximately 20. The historical PE ratio is 15.51. Since that 20 PE is about 22 percent above average, it appears as though the U.S. stock market is somewhat overvalued.

In this circumstance, it does not mean that the markets are going to tank tomorrow. What it suggests is that, at some point, the stock market value will revert back to the mean. In plain English, that means that stock prices need to fall to bring the PE ratio back in line with its average.

Will stock prices fall tomorrow? No one knows for certain. That is why, when valuations are significantly above average, it's wise to put new monies into the market gradually.

DOLLAR COST AVERAGE-AUTOMATE BUYING LOW AND SELLING HIGH

When markets are highly valued, dollar cost average (transfer money regularly into your investment portfolio account; weekly, monthly, quarterly, or semiannually) any large sums in order to avoid trying to time the market. Dollar cost averaging yields more shares when prices are lower and fewer when they are higher. It's a systematic way to tilt towards buying when prices are lower.

If you invest regularly in your workplace retirement account, you're already dollar cost averaging.

ARE YOU READY TO INVEST?

Before investing, make sure to get your financial house in order. You don't want to start investing, only to be forced to pull money out of your investment account when you need a new refrigerator. You might be forced to sell shares in your stock index mutual fund at a lower price than when you originally invested.

Take care of these items before investing.

1. **Emergency Fund**: Don't start investing unless you have an emergency fund of at least a few months' expenses built up to cover unforeseen financial upsets. It's no fun to sell shares of a mutual fund to pay for a car repair or medical bill. Keep this ready access money in a savings account, money market account, or U.S. Treasury I bonds.

2. **Do you have an uncertain income stream?** If your future income is unstable, build up a larger savings cushion before investing. You don't want to be caught short of cash and forced to sell stock or bond funds during a market decline because a freelance job falls through.

3. **How much credit card debt do you have?** If you have a lot of high interest credit card debt, you'll get a better return on your money if you pay off your debt first. (Except if your employer offers a retirement fund match, in that case, invest the amount necessary in the retirement fund in order to get the free money.)

4. **Don't forget about the kids.** Is someone depending upon your income, such as a child or spouse? If so, buy inexpensive term life and disability insurance before investing.

If you're not ready to invest yet, continue learning about investing, and get your financial house in order.

SUMMARY

✓ Investing in financial markets is a strategy to take part of your current earnings and grow them for the future.

✓ Investing is only for money you don't need for at least five years. Financial markets are too volatile for funds you need in the next few years.

✓ Develop basic money and investing knowledge to make wise financial decisions.

✓ Save for an emergency fund and get rid of consumer debt now, before investing.

Chapter 3:
Do You Need An Advisor?

"It's not how much money you make, but how much money you keep, how hard it works for you, and how many generations you keep it for."

Robert Kiyosaki

Some people don't like to deal with money, are afraid of making a mistake and want to turn their financial future over to someone else.

Does that sound like you?

If you choose to hire an advisor, you pay for that advice. And that's money which isn't going to work for you in the financial markets. So be very clear about whether you would prefer to spend a few hours learning the basics of investing or pay from .25% to 1.25% of your assets (or more) to have someone handle your money affairs.

Even if you're apprehensive about handling your own financial affairs, you may be surprised to find that it is easier than you think to manage your own money.

This chapter answers the question, "Do you need an advisor?" as well as explains the various types of financial advisors.

My first experience with an 'advisor', well actually he was a stock broker, was in my 20's. I inherited a small sum of money from my aunt and I planned on investing it. I received a 'cold call' from Brian (not his real name), a stock broker from Prudential Bache Securities (now called Prudential), and we started talking. He was a former biology Ph.D. who made the switch from academia to investments. I was impressed by his educational background and demeanor.

Next, we set up a meeting at his office.

As a side note, this is not the way to choose a financial advisor.

What went wrong with this situation?

I didn't know much about investing, just that it was a good place to put money if you wanted that money to compound and grow. I was leaning more toward bond investments as I thought they were 'safer'.

Brian and I were talking during the early 1980s, a time when the bond returns, based upon Barclay's Aggregate Bond Index (a proxy for the bond market), were quite high.

Notice in this chart that, during the first five years of the 80s, bond returns ranged from 2.71% on up to 32.65% in 1982. (I'd be remiss if I didn't at least mention that inflation was also high during the 1980s so the 'real return', or return after deducting the inflation percent, was much lower.)

Bond Returns 1980-1985	
Year	Barclay's Aggregate Bond Index
1980	2.71%
1981	6.26%
1982	32.65%
1983	8.19%
1984	15.15%
1985	22.13%

I remember to this day the investments he recommended, a closed end bond mutual fund, a GNMA fund (a pool of bonds comprised of mortgage loans whose repayment is guaranteed by the government), and a zero coupon bond (A bond bought at a discount with full value received at maturity. The return is the difference between the purchase price and final maturity value). With high interest rates at this time, and my commitment to hold the investments until maturity, my returns were quite good.

As inflation declined over the years, I locked in the higher bond yields.

So what was the problem?

Brian seemed like a nice guy, he answered my questions, explained dollar cost averaging to me, and even loaned me his investing training materials.

It wasn't until many years later that I recognized the problem with this particular relationship. **The only time Brian was paid was when I bought or sold an investment security.**

Brian was best compensated when I bought investments with higher commissions. The Closed End bond fund was a proprietary product of Prudential Bache Securities, thus Brian probably received a bonus plus commission for peddling that product.

I didn't know the commission on the zero coupon bond because it was embedded in the price.

The GNMA fund also garnered Brian a nice commission.

Finally, he did little to educate me about the importance of diversification across various asset classes, such as stocks, bonds, and cash.

Did I make money with those investments?

Yes, I compounded my initial wealth because I reinvested my dividends and the returns were quite healthy.

If I made money, what was the problem?

I didn't understand that I overpaid for the investments, in the way of large commissions.

> I would have made more money if I'd purchased no load index mutual funds on my own.

The main reason I made money was that I started investing early, and, in spite of the fact that these initial investments weren't optimal, I've been invested for decades.

By beginning to invest in my early 20s, the initial and subsequent investments had time to grow and compound.

Two important takeaways from this first dive into the investing waters were:

1. **Fees matter.** The first question to ask an advisor is, "How are you compensated?" The response lets you know where the advisor's loyalty lies. If the advisor gets paid by commission, they have motivation to sell you products.
2. **Time in the markets is vital.** The longer your money grows, compounds, and makes money on top of the original investment, the greater your ultimate wealth.

TAKE A QUIZ TO DECIDE WHETHER YOU NEED AN ADVISOR OR NOT

Following are two sets of questions. Your answers will help determine whether you need an advisor or not.

WHAT IS AN ADVISOR?

There are many flavors of advisors from which to choose. In general, a financial advisor provides advice to customers in exchange for compensation. You pay an advisor for his or her advice.

Advisors provide various services including investment portfolio management, tax, retirement, insurance, and estate planning. The key job of a planner is to grow the net worth of their clients.

Types of Financial Advisors

There is a dizzying array of financial advisors with an alphabet soup of designations. To further confuse the consumer, various types of advisors have differing levels of experience and expertise. Following are a few of the most popular types of designations:

1. **Certified Financial Planner (CFP)** - The study for this all inclusive designation covers hundreds of financial planning areas. To obtain a CFP, the advisor must pass an examination and complete several years of related work.

2. **Chartered Financial Analyst (CFA)** - This elite designation requires three examinations and work experience. The CFA is competent in accounting, ethics, economics, portfolio management, and securities analysis.

3. **Chartered Financial Consultant (ChFC)** - The ChFC passes an examination covering financial planning, income tax, insurance, investment and estate planning. These advisors must also work three years before obtaining the designation.

HOW MUCH DOES AN ADVISOR COST?

There are four general types of compensation for advisors; commission, hourly, fee for service, or percent of assets under management.

Stock or Investment Broker - This individual is paid by commission. When you buy or sell a security or fund, they receive a commission. Brian, my first stock broker, was paid by commission. There is an inherent conflict of interest in this arrangement because your financial interest is not aligned with that of the advisor. The broker is better compensated when you trade more frequently, and that may not be the best way to increase your wealth.

Fee Only Financial Planner - This investment advisor is usually paid a percent of assets under management. As she manages more assets, the fee usually declines. Fees can range from 1.5% on down to 0.50% of assets under management. Normally, you need a large portfolio in the neighborhood of middle six figures in order to be advised by this type of individual.

This independent fee only financial planner is legally required to act as a fiduciary and must put the clients' interests first.

Fee for Service - Some financial advisors work on a fee for service basis. For example, if you would like someone to review your investments or create a financial plan, the planner would charge an hourly or fee for service rate.

Online Technology Enhanced Financial Advisor - Recently, many varieties of online automated financial advisors (sometimes labeled 'robo advisors') have sprung up. Liz Moyer of the *Wall Street Journal*, wrote a comprehensive article, "Taking Stock of Automated Advisers"[1], about the ins and outs of turning your portfolio over to an online advisor. This cadre of investment managers use computer programs to manage portfolios, at a discount to traditional financial advisors.

These online investment guides differ based upon level and type of services offered as well as fee or commission structure. The online advisor's fees range from zero, for small sums of money on up.

If you fall somewhere in between a 'do it yourselfer' and an "'I need some guidance'" investor, then the technology assisted advisor may be a good choice for you. As with any professional counselor, do your due diligence before you select a company to oversee your money.

WILL I MAKE MORE MONEY WITH A FINANCIAL ADVISOR?

That depends. If you follow the guidelines in the upcoming chapters, invest in low cost index funds in line with your risk tolerance, you may do better on your own. You'll also avoid taking on an extra layer of fees.

On the other hand, if you are subject to fear, anxiety, and worry when you see your investment portfolio value go down and might sell your financial assets at the first sign of a market drop, and subsequently buy in at a market peak, then an advisor might be a good option for you. The right advisor can help you stick with a plan, and keep you from selling on the dips and buying on the peaks.

SUMMARY

✓ A financial advisor gives investing and money advice, recommendation, and management in exchange for a fee.

✓ There are various types of financial advisor qualifications which require differing levels of experience and education.

✓ Financial advisors offer a variety of services and fee structures.

✓ You need to understand how the advisor is compensated. Understand whether the advisor makes money by selling you investment products, the size of your account or a combination of both.

Chapter 4:
Are You a Risk Taker or a Risk Avoider?

"There are two kinds of investors, be they large or small: those who don't know where the market is headed, and those who don't know that they don't know."

William Bernstein, *The Intelligent Asset Allocator*

No one knows where the market is headed. To ward against the uncertain financial markets, know yourself. The financial markets go up and down, and you don't want to jump out at the bottom and in at the top.

UNDERSTAND RISK TOLERANCE AND RISK CAPACITY FOR INVESTING SUCCESS

That's where risk tolerance and risk capacity come in.

There are many risk tolerance quizzes online, all promising to tell you how much volatility you can tolerate. The truth is, no one minds when their portfolio value increases.

> The only risk we care about is the risk that our investments will decline in value.

The risk tolerance quizzes only take you so far. You may think you can handle a 20 percent drop in your portfolio, if you've never experienced one. The only way you know your risk tolerance for certain is to watch the value of your investment portfolio decline and monitor your reaction.

RISK TOLERANCE VERSUS RISK CAPACITY

Michael Kitces, a well-known financial advisor and researcher, wrote about breaking down the risk tolerance concept into two parts; risk tolerance and risk capacity in "Separating Risk Tolerance from Risk Capacity – Just because You Can Afford Risk Doesn't Mean You Should" on *Nerd's Eye View-Kitces Blog*. Traditionally, 'risk tolerance' was the only metric discussed during the 'risk' conversation. As the following 'risk tolerance' quiz shows, this concept attempts to measure how you will react to a decline in your investment portfolio's value.

This newer concept, 'risk capacity' addresses whether you can financially pursue your goals should your portfolio value drop.

Let's look at A.J.'s situation. He has a $2,000,000 investment portfolio, and only needs $25,000 income per year. The rest of A.J.'s retirement income comes from Social Security and a small pension. A.J. is extremely afraid of risk (risk averse). A.J. has a low risk tolerance, because he can't stomach a large decline in his investment portfolio value. Yet, he has a great risk capacity, because, even if his $2,000,000 portfolio drops in value, he will be able to withdraw $25,000 per year in retirement.

How do you know this?

Twenty-five thousand dollars is only a 1.5% withdrawal rate from a $2,000,000 investment portfolio. Even if the portfolio fell 25% to $1,500,000, a $25,000 annual withdrawal would only be 1.67% of the portfolio's total value; a sustainable amount to take out each year.

To put this in context, many financial professionals suggest that a 3 to 4 percent annual withdrawal rate is sustainable during the retiree's lifetime. A.J.'s needs are well below this benchmark.

With his low risk tolerance and high risk capacity, A.J. is well served to invest in a very conservative investment portfolio.

Conversely, Tiffany has a $250,000 retirement portfolio and hopes to take out $20,000 per year from her investment nest egg. She has a high risk tolerance and can accept swings in value in her investment portfolio.

What is Tiffany's risk capacity?

Tiffany has a low risk capacity, in fact, she has unreasonable expectations about her portfolio. If she withdraws $20,000 from a $250,000 retirement portfolio, that's equal to an 8% withdrawal rate. At that rate, her retirement nest egg will most likely run out before her life ends.

Even in a best case scenario, with an aggressive allocation of 70% stock; 30% bond portfolio, the retirement money is unlikely to withstand her aggressive $20,000 annual extraction expectations.

In a down year, Tiffany's investments might fall 25 percent, reducing her investment net worth to $187,500. Take $20,000 from this and Tiffany is facing a 10.67 percent withdrawal rate. Definitely unsustainable.

In an up year, Tiffany's investments might rise 25 percent. How would that impact her investment percent withdrawal?

In the golden year, her $250,000 grows to $312,500. Take out $20,000 from this newly inflated nest egg and Tiffany's withdrawal rate of 6.4% is still unsustainable.

Tiffany has a low risk capacity because her next egg is too small to support her withdrawal expectations. Regardless of her risk tolerance, she needs to revise her withdrawal rate in order to preserve her investment portfolio.

WHAT IS YOUR RISK TOLERANCE?

Realistically, you need to go through a bear market or two to find out your true risk tolerance. In the recent 2008- 36.5% stock market drop (as measured by the S & P 500), I saw our investment portfolio fall along with the total U.S. and world markets'. Was I distressed? Of course. Did I sell after the drop? No.

I tend to be an anxious person. I've been that way since childhood, I'm a worrier. In fact, when markets are up, I worry about how long the bull market will last and when prices will fall.

When the markets correct and drop in value for a year or more, I worry about whether they will ever go back up again. Yet, I've learned not to respond or act upon my anxiety.

How do I ignore my fears and remain disciplined during market swings?

The tactics that've helped me build wealth and stay the course throughout the market ups and downs are knowledge and understanding of how financial markets have behaved in the past as well as what drives stock prices. So, even though I'm a worrier by nature, I'm moderately risk tolerant and know I can handle the inherent volatility in the financial markets.

By understanding the cyclical nature of the economy and stock prices, it's easier to withstand the inevitable market troughs.

In the meantime, take the following Sleep at Night Guide to Risk© quiz to get an idea of your risk tolerance.

This simple quiz gives you an idea of how much downward risk you can tolerate in your investment portfolio.

PUTTING RISK TOLERANCE AND RISK CAPACITY INTO ACTION

Calculating your risk tolerance is an inexact science. You may feel differently on various days about one level of risk or another. The important thing is to create a 'ballpark' asset allocation that reflects your risk tolerance. (Asset allocation is the percent of your investment dollars that goes into stock versus fixed funds.)

Fortunately, most investment portfolios' returns are smoothed out with a combination of stock and fixed investments. That way, even if the stock portion of your portfolio falls -25% the bond portion might increase, and thus your overall portfolio value will decline less than 25%.

With a 60% stock; 40% bond portfolio, when the stock market drops -25% and the bond market returns +3%, your total investment portfolio only drops -13.8%. No one's shouting, "Great, I only lost -13.8% last year," but a -13.8% nest egg decline is better than a -25% fall in an all stock risky portfolio.

And that is why you want a diversified portfolio!

In my mid 20's, I was terrified of risk. Even though I was young and had many years until retirement, I was afraid that if I invested in the stock market it would crash—like it did in 1929, and I would lose all my money.

Add to that fear the fact that I had no idea about stock and bond market history or characteristics.

Do you have those same fears about losing money?

Are you afraid that, if you invest, you'll make a mistake, do it wrong, and lose all of your money?

That's why you start with a quiz about your risk tolerance. If you have a low risk tolerance and will go nuts with the slightest drop in value, then you want to make sure to have an investment portfolio with more bond assets than stocks. And understand that you are a 'conservative' investor.

But, as we discussed at the beginning of the chapter, don't forget about risk capacity. After you have a ballpark of your risk tolerance, think about your risk capacity. In general, if you're young and saving for retirement, you have a large risk capacity. If your investment values tank, you have decades to make up the losses.

If you're staring down the barrel of retirement, need $30,000 annually in retirement, and your nest egg is smaller than $750,000 (4% withdrawal rate from a $750,000 portfolio is $30,000), then you have a lower 'risk capacity'.

To better understand the concepts of risk, let's look at four investors' situations.

Jamie's Asset Allocation and Risk Profile

Consider Jamie, your 30-year-old neighbor, who is okay with a 30% drop in his investments one year, because he understands that he has a long time to make up that loss. Jamie's a more aggressive investor and can handle a greater percent of his investment portfolio in stock funds.

Esther's Asset Allocation and Risk Profile

Esther is 55 and looking to retire at age 65. She is more concerned with keeping the value of her investments steady.

She doesn't want any surprises in her retirement nest egg now. Esther is a conservative investor and has 40% in stock investments, 40% in bond investments and 20% in cash.

Her portfolio value is on track to meet her withdrawal requirements. Thus, both her risk tolerance and risk capacity are conservative.

Julio's Asset Allocation and Risk Profile

Julio is 45 and in his prime earning years. He is consistently contributing to his 401(k) and scored a B on the Sleep at Night Guide to Risk©. Julio's a moderate investor. His asset allocation is 60% stock investments and 40% bond investments. His investment growth will also align his risk tolerance with his risk capacity as long as he keeps adding to his retirement account.

If Julio stops contributing to his 401(k), his retirement account may not have the risk capacity to keep up with his preferred retirement withdrawal amount.

Rose's Asset Allocation and Risk Profile

Rose is 30, married with a small child. Rose is an aggressive investor. Rose and her husband both have good jobs and are maxing out their 401(k) accounts. They have a 7 month emergency fund saved up and can handle some risk in their investment portfolios. Rose owns 70% stock funds and 30% bond funds, this is in line with her aggressive risk tolerance.

With many years until retirement, Rose is invested in line with her age, risk tolerance and risk capacity.

The risk concepts aren't stagnant and investors need to reevaluate their risk picture every decade or so.

You may think that all older people are conservative investors and younger adults are more aggressive investors, but that's not true. There are other factors at play when considering one's risk tolerance and asset allocation. When you set up your asset allocation take these aspects into consideration, along with your risk tolerance:

- Is your job stable? If so, you can afford more risk in your asset allocation.

- Do you have a large enough cash cushion to handle potential emergencies? Six to nine months' salary is a good target. If not, you want to focus on saving up your 'emergency cash' before (or in tandem with) investing.

- Do you foresee large expenses soon? Are you saving for a down payment on a home or college for an older child? If so, don't put any of the money you need within the next five years in the stock market. Keep it in 'cash' investments.

SUMMARY

✓ Before investing a dime in the stock and bond markets, understand yourself. Think about how you will respond to the inevitable drops in stock and bond prices.

✓ If you can't sleep at night with a large drop in your investment portfolio, then you are a conservative investor. Conservative investors hold a greater percentage of bonds and cash in their investment portfolios and a smaller percentage of stocks.

✓ Consider time until retirement when investing. In general, if you are closer to retirement, you may want a more conservative investment portfolio.

✓ Understand your risk capacity. If you have a greater amount saved for retirement, your risk capacity is also larger, and vice versa.

Don't worry if you're uncertain about the best asset allocation for you. You can start with one asset allocation between stocks and fixed assets and adjust your investment proportions along the way.

Chapter 5:
Which Investments Go in Your Portfolio?

"The individual investor should act consistently as an investor and not as a speculator."

Benjamin Graham

MUTUAL FUND OVERLOAD

How many mutual funds do you think there are?

One hundred? One thousand? Ten thousand?

According to the 2014 Investment Company Fact Book[1], there are 7,707 mutual funds with 264.8 million shareholders. This is up from 68 mutual funds in 1940 and 296 thousand shareholder accounts.

You could go out of your mind trying to choose a fund from among thousands. That's why sticking with a simple, index fund approach, with a limited number of asset classes, not only simplifies your investing, but also beats the returns of the majority of active mutual fund managers.

Barry Schwartz, psychologist and author of *The Paradox of Choice,* claims that consumers actually respond better to fewer choices rather than more. He tells of a famous research experiment by Professor Iyengar of Columbia University. Iyengar and his associates set up a jam stand in a California gourmet market. During the experiment they switched the display of jam every few hours from a group of six jams to a selection of 24.

Iyengar found that, on average, each customer tasted approximately two jams, regardless of the size of the display. Each visitor received a $1.00 off coupon, good for a jam purchase.

Here's how the story ended.

Sixty percent of the customers stopped by the large assortment and only forty percent stopped by the small one; so more shoppers were enticed by the larger selection. But the percent of actual buyers did not continue on that same track.

Thirty percent of the shoppers who sampled from the small selection decided to buy. Whereas, only three percent of those faced with the 24 jar display actually bought a jar of jam.

What does this example tell you?

In the abstract, we like the idea of many choices. But, in reality we are paralyzed by too much choice and prefer a smaller selection from which to choose. The large selection encouraged browsers, but after looking at and sampling the large display, most shoppers were too overwhelmed to buy.

Don't let this same situation keep you from investing.

Are you feeling overwhelmed by the abundance of investing choices?

Don't worry, you can successfully ignore most of the funds and stick with the plain vanilla, low cost, index funds offered by your retirement and discount brokerage firms.

To keep the fear at bay, in this chapter, you'll get a narrowed down sample of mutual funds from which to choose. And based on reams of investment research, I'm certain that you'll have enough mutual funds to create an investment portfolio which will beat most active mutual fund managers. Not only will it be easier to set up the portfolio, but over time, you'll be able to manage your own investments efficiently.

If for some reason, your discount investment firm or workplace 401(k) or 403(b) retirement plan's funds aren't listed, don't worry. As long as the expense ratios (listed in the fund prospectus) are less than 0.5% for the available index funds, you'll be fine. (An international index fund might have an expense ratio a bit higher.)

WHAT IS AN INDEX FUND?

An index fund is a proxy for a current market index. Index fund discussions are all over the media. But what exactly does index mean?

The stock market is categorized into a variety of groups, called indexes. These categories are helpful in analyzing market behavior. The most popular index and the one used most often to represent the total stock market is the Standard and Poor's 500 or S & P 500. This index contains 500 of the most widely held stocks and attempts to represent the total U.S. stock market in proportion to their market capitalization (or number of shares multiplied by share price).

Apart from the S & P 500, the world of indexes and their accompanying funds expands to include many configurations of sections of the markets such as small capitalization, developing world markets, value, health care, technology, and many more index funds. Some of these types of funds mirror a particular market sector, such as banking or precious metals. Others represent a certain investing style such as growth, value stocks, developing international nations, or small capitalization stocks.

There are bond market index funds too. You'll find government bond index funds along with broadly diversified corporate or total bond market index funds. The diversified bond funds may hold various types of corporate bonds, government bonds, and other issues as well. Junk bond funds offer investors a higher yield for a greater risk.

For every popular market index there are one or more mutual funds and ETFs designed to mirror the particular indexes' holdings and returns.

In spite of the multitude of index mutual funds, it's quite easy to narrow down the index fund universe and choose a few for your portfolio.

In the vast world of index funds, you decide how simple or how complex you want your investment portfolio to be.

For the minimalist, a two fund portfolio consisting of one total world stock index fund (such as Vanguard Total World Stock Index Fund-VTWSX) and one total bond market index fund (such as Vanguard Total Bond Market Index Fund-VBMFX) might be enough.

One can obtain a diversified portfolio with as few as two or three index funds.

For those who desire a more exhaustive diversification, a portfolio of eight to ten or more index funds is possible. After a certain point, it's debatable how much diversification benefit there is to adding more funds.

INDEX MUTUAL FUND AND INDEX EXCHANGE TRADED FUND (ETF) DRILL DOWN

Now that you understand the ins and outs of an index fund, let's break down two types of funds; index mutual fund and exchange traded fund (ETF).

What is the difference between an index mutual fund and an index exchange traded fund (ETF)?

You may have wondered about ETFs and how they differ from a typical index mutual fund. First off, think of both mutual funds and ETFs as baskets that hold individual stocks, bonds, or a combination of both.

An S & P 500 Index mutual fund can hold the exact same underlying 500 stocks as an S & P Index ETF.

With the mutual fund, you buy the shares directly from the issuing company, such as Vanguard, Fidelity, or Schwab.

The price you pay is the net asset value (NAV) at the end of the trading day. The price is set one time per day.

In contrast, an ETF is bought from another investor. Although originally set up by an investment company, the ETF ultimately trades on public financial markets, similar to a stock. So, when you buy 100 shares of VTI, the Vanguard Total Stock Market ETF at 2:00 pm on Tuesday, you're buying from another investor who is selling those shares.

When you buy the ETF within your investment brokerage account there may or may not be a commission (depends on the investment brokerage company and the offering fund family of the ETF). For example, Schwab and many other fund families sell their own index ETFs commission free.

ETFs are priced throughout the day and the price is based upon supply and demand. That's why an ETF may sell at a premium or discount to its net asset value (NAV), or the value of its underlying securities.

Although there are many varieties of both mutual funds and ETFs, this book focuses only on those funds which follow a widely accepted index. The decision whether to buy an index mutual fund or an exchange traded fund will be determined by availability (for example, in a retirement account), commissions, and management fees. An S & P 500 index mutual fund and ETF are, essentially, the same.

Now, we'll narrow down your investment choices. Let's slash the thousands of funds down to a more targeted list.

WHICH ARE THE BEST INDEX FUNDS?

Many investment companies offer the same type of index funds. For example, there are S & P 500 index funds sponsored by Vanguard, Fidelity, Schwab and others. There's little difference among the funds.

The best index funds closely track the returns of their underlying index and charge low fees. Don't get fooled by funds that have index in their title but aren't. We'll talk about enhanced index funds later in the chapter. On a side note, 'enhanced' doesn't mean 'better'.

Here's an example of a very basic three index fund portfolio.

3 Asset Class Index Fund Portfolio-60% Stocks: 40% Bonds

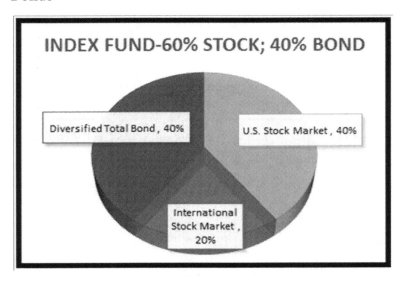

3 Asset Class Diversified Portfolio

This simple 3 asset class portfolio has sufficient diversification. It covers U.S. and international stocks as well as bonds (fixed asset class).

Most moderately conservative investors could set up and manage this portfolio and obtain successful market matching returns. The ten year return[2] from November 11, 2005 through November 10, 2014 of this portfolio was 6.36% [(.40 x .0839) + (.20 x .0591) + (.40 x .0456)].

A $10,000 investment in this three asset class portfolio would have grown to $18,526 over the last ten years.

The other end of the spectrum is the following complex diversified asset classes investment portfolio.

11 Asset Class Index Fund Portfolio-60% Stocks: 40% Bonds

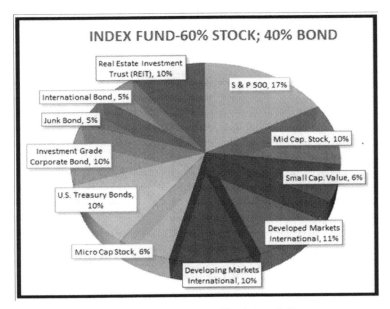

11 Asset Class Diversified Portfolio

This eleven asset class portfolio is fine, but there is no guarantee it'll perform any better than a three index fund portfolio. And if it does outperform in one period, you can't be certain that the more complicated portfolio will continue to beat the 3 asset class portfolio.

Which is preferable; few or many asset classes?

It depends on how much management and oversight you prefer. The number of asset classes in your investment portfolio is your decision. There's no right answer and you may boost your returns and reduce risk a bit with more index funds, but it's not guaranteed.

"It's possible—even at times desirable—to construct a very well-diversified portfolio using just three low-cost mutual funds or ETFs", wrote Anna Prior in the *Wall Street Journal* article, "A Portfolio That's as Simple as One, Two, Three"[2].

WHERE TO BUY INDEX FUNDS

Almost every large discount brokerage company offers a stable of index funds. The brand or company doesn't make much difference. For example, if your investment brokerage account is with Fidelity, then you may want to look at the Fidelity index mutual funds.

Most workplace retirement 401(k) or 403(b) plans offer a few index funds.

Morningstar.com[3] is a great resource to use when investigating and selecting mutual funds. Morningstar has a free and paid version (with a two week free trial).

Although, in most cases, the issuing fund family doesn't matter, expenses do. Be sure to check the annual expense ratio for the index fund before you invest. In general, most index mutual funds charge a fee which ranges from 0.09 percent to 0.65 percent of the total amount invested in the fund.

You can find a total U.S. stock market index fund ETF (VTI) with a rock bottom annual fee of 0.05 percent. Imagine saving 0.29 percent every year, just by choosing a lower cost fund. Over years, along with a growing portfolio, this small fee difference can add thousands of dollars to your nest egg.

ASSET CLASSES AND INDEX FUND INVESTING-"WHAT SHOULD I INVEST IN?"

Following are popular asset classes with sample index mutual funds and ETFs for each category. This section will help narrow down your index fund choices. It'll also clear up that question so commonly posed, "What should I invest in?"

These index and exchange traded funds are examples to consider when choosing specific funds. In most cases, there isn't much difference between the Fidelity, Schwab, iShares, Vanguard, or other comparable index mutual and ETF fund families.

Sample Index Funds and ETFs by Asset Class

EQUITY ASSET CLASS INDEX FUNDS

Stock Market Index Funds

Total U.S. Stock Market

Schwab Total Stock Market Index Fund (SWTX)
Vanguard Total Stock Market Index Fund (Investor Shares) (VTSMX)

U.S. Large Capitalization U.S. Stock Market Index Funds

Fidelity Spartan 500 Index Fund (FUSEX)
Vanguard 500 Index (VFINX)

Small Capitalization U.S. Stock Market Index Funds

iShares Russell 2000 ETF (IWM)
Vanguard Small Cap Index (NAESX)

International Stock Market Index Funds

Vanguard Total World Stock Index Fund Investor Shares (VTWSX)
Vanguard Total World Stock ETF (VT)
Vanguard FTSE All World ex-US Index Fund Investor Shares (VFWIX)
Fidelity Spartan International Index Fund Investor Class (FSIIX)

Developed Market International Index Funds

Schwab International Equity ETF (SCHF)
iShares Core MSCI EAFE (IEFA)

Emerging Markets International Index Funds

Vanguard International Equity Index Fund Emerging Markets (VEIEX)
Vanguard FTSE Emerging Markets ETF (VWO)

FIXED ASSET CLASS INDEX FUNDS

Bond Market Index Funds

Total Bond Market Index Funds

Vanguard Total Bond Market Index Fund (VBTLX)
iShares Core Total US Bond Market ETF (AGG)

Corporate Bond Index Funds

Vanguard Intermediate-Term Corporate Bond Index Fund Admiral Shares (VICSX)
Vanguard Short-Term Corporate Bond Index Fund Admiral Shares (VSCSX)
Short-Term Corporate Bond Index ETF (BMO)

Inflation Protected Bond Funds

Fidelity Inflation-Protected Bond Index Fund (FSIPX)
Treasury Inflation Protected Securities ETF (TIP)

International Bond Fund

PowerShares International Corporate Bond ETF (PICB)

Real Estate Index Funds

U.S. and International Real Estate Index Funds

Vanguard REIT ETF (VNQ)
SPDR Dow Jones International Real Estate ETF (RWX)

Are these all the available index mutual fund asset class categories? No.

If you want to get fancy, you can drill down into even more asset classes for your investment portfolio.

Do you need a fund from each of these categories?

Absolutely not. As we've discussed, you can design a successful investment portfolio with as few as three index funds.

Personally, since the only real estate our family currently owns is our own home, I like to include some additional exposure to real estate by owning a real estate investment trust (REIT) fund. This is a personal preference and not an investing requirement.

In reality, there's no reason to over diversify. The evidence doesn't validate that more asset classes leads to greater returns.

TIPS FOR INDEX INVESTING

Smart investors understand that fees matter. The lower the management fee charged by the index mutual or exchange traded fund, the greater percent of your money is invested and working for you.

When you pay a fee greater than 1.0 percent for a mutual fund, then that fund must earn 1.0 percent before you see any return on your investment.

Fees vary for all mutual funds. Expect to pay a low of 0.05 percent fee for a rock bottom index fund to 1.3 percent or more for an actively managed mutual fund. Low fees are one of the reasons index funds are such a wise investing choice.

Check how closely the index mutual fund tracks its underlying index. If the Vanguard Total Stock Market ETF (VTI) purports to track the Dow Jones Total U.S. Stock Market Index then the ETF's return should be very close to that of the Dow Jones Total U.S. Stock Market Index.

The difference between the ETF's return and that of the index is usually explained by the index fund's management fee. So, if the fund charges a 0.05% management fee and the Dow Jones Total U.S. Stock Market Index period return is 10.00% then the Vanguard Total Stock Market ETF's (VTI) return should be close to 9.95% (10.00% - 0.05%).

Be aware that some index funds aren't true index funds. With the quest to develop more investment products, some mutual funds with the term 'index' in their title aren't true index funds. 'Enhanced index funds' seek to beat their underlying indexes by using various strategies. Some 'enhanced index funds' use derivatives to try to beat the index; others invest the cash in the fund in higher yielding investments.

The enhanced index funds are veiled actively managed funds without enough evidence to confirm their superiority to traditional index mutual funds or ETFs.

Confused by which S & P 500 or total bond index fund to choose? It's an easy choice, either choose the one available in your workplace retirement account, or the one with the lowest expense ratio.[4]

If your investment brokerage account is held with Fidelity, use their low cost index funds when constructing your portfolio. If your 401(k) offers Vanguard funds, then choose the Vanguard fund offerings in your retirement account. Keep your investing simple.

SUMMARY

✓ An index fund is a proxy for a current market index. One of the most common stock index funds is an S & P 500 index mutual, or exchange traded fund. This type of fund is available from a variety of fund families.

✓ Mutual funds and exchange traded funds can both copy the same index. Mutual funds are bought from the fund family or investment brokerage company and are priced once daily. ETFs trade on stock exchanges like stocks.

✓ An investment portfolio includes a variety of index mutual funds. You can obtain adequate diversification with as few as three mutual funds or ETFs.

✓ To simplify investing and still beat most active fund managers' returns, narrow your fund universe.

✓ Choose index funds based upon availability in your retirement account, fees, and how well the fund matches its underlying index.

Chapter 6:
Blueprint for an Index Fund Portfolio
(FOR YOUR RISK LEVEL)
THAT BEATS THE PROS

"Investing should be more like watching paint dry or watching grass grow. If you want excitement, take $800 and go to Las Vegas."

Paul Samuelson

You have the tools to put the plan into action.

You understand your risk tolerance, from the Sleep at Night Guide to Risk © in Chapter 4. You've learned how to winnow down the list of available index funds to a manageable number.

When setting up your investment portfolio, keep in mind these asset classes characteristics:

1. Stocks and stock index mutual funds usually yield higher returns along with greater risk.

2. Fixed index mutual funds usually have lower returns and less risk or volatility.

SAMPLE DIVERSIFIED PORTFOLIOS FOR VARIOUS RISK LEVELS

Most of the following sample portfolios have a maximum of four asset classes. If you are comfortable with more asset classes and willing to spend additional time managing them, you can add more specialization.

First, you'll see three basic risk profiles; Low Risk Tolerant-Conservative, Medium Risk Tolerant-Moderate, and High Risk Tolerant-Aggressive. For each risk level, there are several portfolio alternatives. These are provided to give you a vision of how your portfolio may appear.

Investing is both an art than a science, so the savvy investor understands that these portfolios are a guide not a mandate.

The following sample portfolios are an educational tool to help you visualize how a particular investment portfolio would be constructed. They are not a prescription for exactly how to invest.

Who is the Low Risk Tolerant-Conservative Investor?

You are either near or in retirement or extremely uncomfortable with the ups and downs in your financial portfolio.

Your investments will include more fixed assets and fewer stock investments than the more aggressive portfolios.

As previously mentioned, each asset class lists sample index or exchange traded funds, there's no need to use the exact fund, a comparable one is fine.

Use the approximate percentages allocated to stock, bond, and cash asset classes as your guide.

1. Conservative Portfolio-50% Stocks: 50% Fixed

25% U.S. short-term bond fund – Vanguard Short-term Bond Index (VBISX)

25% Inflation protected fund – iShares TIPS Bond ETF (TIP) or iShares 0-5 TIPS Bond (STIP)

50% All world stock fund – Vanguard Total World Stock Index ETF (VT)

This portfolio has 50% allocated to stocks and 50% invested in bond type investments. The Vanguard Total World Stock Index ETF is a proxy for the entire world stock market. It's a great choice if you're looking for one fund to cover your complete stock market allocation, U. S. and international.

2. Conservative Portfolio-40% Stocks: 60% Fixed

30% Cash – Certificate of deposits (CD), money market mutual funds

30% Inflation protected fund[1]– Buy individual I Bonds at Treasurydirect.gov and/or iShares TIPS Bond ETF (TIP) or iShares 0-5 TIPS Bond (STIP)

40% All world stock fund – Vanguard Total World Stock Index ETF (VT)

The second conservative portfolio invests 40%, a lesser and more conservative allocation to U.S. and international stocks. This ultra conservative portfolio is suitable for a conservative retiree investor. Thirty percent of the assets are invested in the ultra-safe inflation protected government bond category with 30% in cash assets.

3. Conservative Portfolio-40% Stocks: 60% Fixed

60% Short-term bond fund – Vanguard Short-term Bond Index (VBISX)

27% Total U.S. stock market fund– Vanguard Total Stock Market Index (VTSMX)

13% All world (ex-US) stock fund – Vanguard FTSE All World ex-US ETF (VEU)

The third conservative portfolio invests 27% in U.S. stocks, 13% in international stocks, with 60% in short-term U.S. bonds. This might be an appropriate portfolio for the older investor in the beginning stages of retirement. Declines in the stock market at the beginning stages of retirement can devastate a retiree's nest egg.

Who is the Medium Risk Tolerant-Moderate Investor?

You might be any age. You understand investment markets are cyclical. You are aware that your portfolio might go down 20 or 25 percent one year, but that over the long-term it is likely to increase in value.

Your portfolio will have a moderate amount of both stock investments and fixed investments. You could be any age.

1. Moderate Portfolio-60% Stocks: 40% Fixed

20% U.S. short-term bond fund – Vanguard Short-term Bond Index (VBISX)

20% Inflation protected fund – iShares TIPS Bond ETF (TIP) or iShares 0-5 TIPS Bond (STIP)

60% All world stock fund – Vanguard Total World Stock Index ETF (VT)

This moderate portfolio - 60% stock fund and 40% fixed is a customary asset allocation. The bond or fixed portion is divided between short-term and inflation protected bonds, a relatively conservative fixed asset choice. The addition of a longer term bond fund would make this particular portfolio more aggressive.

2. Moderate Portfolio-60% Stocks: 40% Fixed

20% Diversified Bond Fund – Vanguard Total Bond Market Index Fund Investor Shares (VBMFX)

10% Inflation protected fund – Buy individual I Bonds at Treasurydirect.gov and/or iShares TIPS Bond ETF (TIP) or iShares 0-5 TIPS Bond (STIP)

10% International bond fund – iShares Core MSCI Total International Stock ETF (IXUS)

10% - Large capitalization value fund – iShares Russell 1000 Value ETF (IWD)

30%-Total U.S. stock market index fund – Spartan Total Market Index Fund (FSTMX)

20% All world (ex-US) stock fund – Vanguard FTSE All World ex-US Stock Index

This portfolio is similar to the first moderate portfolio in that they both invest 60% in stocks and 40% in bonds, yet instead of only two funds, this portfolio adds a bit more diversification with an international bond fund. The diversified bond fund covers most of the U.S. bond market. The I bonds (or TIPS) are issued by the government and protect the investor's principal from inflation.

The stock portion of this portfolio includes an international index fund, a U.S. index fund, and 10% in a large cap value fund. The large cap value fund invests in undervalued stocks and hopes to capitalize on the 'market anomaly' indicating that undervalued assets tend to outperform the indexes. The international stock arena is taken care of with the all world, ex-U.S. fund.

3. Moderate Portfolio-55% Stocks: 45% Fixed

45% Short-term bond fund – Vanguard Short-term Bond Index (VBISX)

10% REIT fund– iShares U.S. Real Estate Index (IYR)

25% Total U.S. stock market fund – Vanguard Total Stock Market Index (VTSMX)

20% All world (ex-U.S.) stock fund – Vanguard FTSE All World ex-U.S. Stock Index (VFWIX)

Although this portfolio has fewer assets allocated to stocks and a greater percent to bonds, it is still considered a moderately conservative portfolio.

The 10% invested in the real estate investment trust (REIT) adds the real estate asset class to the diversification mix. This portfolio might be a good choice for someone who doesn't own a home or any other real estate.

Who is the High Risk Tolerant-Aggressive Investor?

You understand that in the long-term stocks outperformed all other asset classes. You are confident that, over time, due to growing U.S. and global companies, even large portfolio declines will be offset by increases in value. You might be in your 20s or 30s and realize that, even if your portfolio tanks, you have many working years in which to recoup the losses.

Your portfolio will have more stock investments and fewer fixed investments.

1. Aggressive Portfolio-70% Stocks: 30% Fixed

30% Short-term bond fund – Vanguard Short-term Bond Index (VBISX)

35% Total U.S. stock market fund – Vanguard Total Stock Market Index (VTSMX)

25% All world (ex-U.S.) stock fund – Vanguard FTSE All World ex-U.S. Stock Index (VFWIX)

10% US REIT fund – iShares U.S. Real Estate Index (IYR)

Notice that this aggressive portfolio holds the exact same funds as the third moderate portfolio. The only difference between the two is the allocations to stock and fixed assets. Stocks are riskier with the possibility of higher returns, so the more aggressive investor will choose a portfolio with a greater chance of outsized returns.

2. Aggressive Portfolio-80% Stocks: 20% Fixed

10% U.S. short-term bond fund – Vanguard Short-term Bond Index (VBISX)

10% Inflation protected fund – iShares TIPS Bond ETF (TIP) or iShares 0-5 TIPS Bond (STIP)

10% International REIT fund – SPDR Dow Jones International Real Estate (RWX)

40% Total U.S. stock market fund – Vanguard Total Stock Market Index (VTSMX)

10% U.S. small cap stock fund – Vanguard Small Cap ETF (VB)

20% All world (ex-U.S.) stock fund – Vanguard FTSE All World ex-U.S. Stock Index

This aggressive portfolio has the same asset allocation as the former but includes six funds instead of four. In addition to the traditional U.S. and international index funds, this aggressive grouping of assets plays on the small cap market anomaly. This well researched theory finds that small capitalization stocks tend to outperform the major market indexes in the long-term.

3. Aggressive Portfolio-75% Stocks: 25% Fixed

15% U.S. short-term bond fund – Vanguard Short-term Bond Index (VBISX)

10% I bonds – Buy individual I Bonds at Treasurydirect.gov and/or iShares TIPS Bond

10% U.S. REIT fund – iShares US Real Estate Index (IYR)

5% International REIT– SPDR Dow Jones International Real Estate (RWX)

30% Total U.S. stock market – Vanguard Total Stock Market Index (VTSMX)

10% U.S. small cap stock fund – Vanguard Small Cap ETF (VB)

10% Developed market international fund – iShares MSCI EAFE (EFA)

10% Emerging markets international fund – Schwab Emerging Markets Equity (SCHE)

This aggressive portfolio is the most diversified of all of the portfolios. Although the broad asset allocation is 75% stocks and 25% fixed; 15% of the stock category is allocated to real estate. Of the real estate allocation, we've included 5% in an international REIT fund.

In addition to the international REIT, the international stock category includes both developed and emerging market funds.

Why would an investor choose this type of allocation? If he or she desires greater international diversification and wants to include international real estate, they might choose this portfolio. This investor may also want to capitalize on the small company anomaly which suggests that smaller companies may grow more quickly and thus offer greater returns than larger firms.

Will this additional diversification improve returns? Only time will tell.

As a side note, the REIT funds can also be included in their own 'real estate' asset class. They are included in the stock category for simplicity's sake and although they pay regular dividend payments, they are considered a stock asset.

BOND CAVEAT

Most bond fund recommendations were short term since interest rates during 2014 and 2015 were at historical lows. Due to the inverse relationship between interest rates and bonds, when interest rates rise, longer term bond funds will lose value.

If you're reading this book at a time when interest rates are more stable and in the normal 3 to 4 percent range, you may want to replace the short term bond funds with intermediate term diversified bond index funds.

HOW MUCH DIVERSIFICATION IS ENOUGH?

Modern portfolio theory suggests that diversification of uncorrelated assets can not only increase returns, but reduce risk or volatility. But how much diversification is truly needed?

Understand that, within one index fund, such as a total all world stock index fund, you'll have hundreds of companies. That's more than enough equity diversification from just one fund. So even with a two fund portfolio (one all world Stock Fund and one diversified Bond Fund), you hold enough individual stocks and bonds to benefit from a diversified portfolio.

The problem with predicting whether more asset classes are better than fewer, is that one asset class might go up handsomely during one decade, only to underperform the following.

Investing is an inexact science. The only part of investing that we understand without fail is the past. Yet, if you believe that United States and global businesses will continue to grow, you will likely profit from investing.

My favorite example of how various index fund portfolios perform over time is shown in these Paul B. Farrell's Lazy Portfolios[2], updated on the *Wall Street Journal*'s MarketWatch.com.

Farrell follows eight diversified index fund investment portfolios. The "Second Grader's Starter" portfolio includes only three funds and the "Aronson Family Taxable" portfolio holds eleven funds in various asset classes.

The website Marketwatch Lazy Portfolio shows one, three, five, and ten year annualized returns for each of the eight 'lazy' index fund portfolios. As of August 27, 2014, the portfolio with the worst ten year return held 9 asset classes and the best performing portfolio held three asset classes.

Yet, if you look at another time period, there will probably be different winning and losing portfolios.

Before you assume that fewer asset classes are better, be aware that there was only a 0.04% difference in return between the 3 and 11 asset class portfolios. And there's no guarantee that the next ten years will have similar returns to the prior ten. In fact, it's quite unlikely.

Before jumping to any conclusions, it is important to consider the overall asset mix between stock and fixed assets. The recent winning 3 asset class lazy portfolio was quite aggressive with a 90% stock and 10% fixed allocation.

SUMMARY

✓ There are approximately 8,000 mutual funds.

✓ Index and Exchange Traded Mutual Funds are constructed to mirror common investment market indexes. These indexes are created to measure the performance of particular segments of the investment world. The S & P 500 is one of the most popular stock market indexes and frequently serves as a proxy for the total U.S. stock market.

✓ The best index funds closely track the composition and returns of their underlying indexes and levy low management fees.

✓ The fund family doesn't matter, most major discount investment brokerage companies offer comparable index funds.

✓ Construct your asset allocation or percent of stock index funds versus bond index funds based upon your risk tolerance. If you're a more aggressive investor, you'll have a larger percent of your total assets invested in stock funds. The more conservative investor will lean towards a greater percent in fixed (cash and bond) investments.

Chapter 7:
Quick Start Guide for a 6-7 Figure Retirement Account

"The secret of getting ahead is getting started."

Mark Twain

By now, you understand why it's advisable to invest in index funds. You also have a good idea about the percentages you'll allocate to stock versus fixed type investments. You've even got sample portfolios to use as a guide. And you remember that only money you won't need for five or more years belongs in the financial markets.

WHERE TO HOUSE LONG-TERM INVESTABLE FUNDS?

But where's all the money going to come from for these investing portfolios? Or, as Jerry Maguire (Tom Cruise) shouted to Rod Tidwell (Cuba Gooding Jr.) in the 1996 movie, *Jerry Maguire*, "Show me the money!"

If your workplace offers a <u>workplace retirement plan</u>[1] such as a 401(K), 403(B), or Roth IRA, where you contribute part of your salary (pretax) and your employer matches a portion of your contribution, then that is where to open your investment account.

The workplace retirement account is the golden gift of investing.

Not only are your funds transferred into the account pretax, but, in most cases, your employer chips in with some free matching cash. It's not unusual for your employer to match up to 5 percent of your salary or even more. So if you make $60,000 per year, that's an extra $3,000 into your retirement account.

Transfer as much as you can into that workplace retirement account. It's preferable to contribute the maximum amount allowable by law. The amount changes periodically, but you can find the annual amount either from your human resources department or the IRS website. If you can't invest the maximum, make sure to **contribute at least enough to get a full employer match.**

The human resources office will tell you how to open the account and start directing your money into the appropriate mutual fund.

If you can't swing the maximum contribution amount, set a goal, such as 10 percent of your gross income. Next, commit to allocating all bonuses and raises to your retirement account. You'll be surprised that, after the initial adjustment, you won't miss the money that you don't see.

HOW TO INVEST IF YOUR WORKPLACE DOESN'T OFFER A RETIREMENT PLAN

If your workplace doesn't offer a retirement plan, open a Roth IRA[2] on your own. If you have self-employment income you can also open a SEP IRA or Solo 401(k)[3]. Open the account at a discount broker such as Charles Schwab,

Fidelity, or Vanguard.

For small amounts, Charles Schwab has a $1,000 investment minimum for most accounts (the minimum opening balance is waived with $100 automatic deposits).

You may not like this, but whether you have a workplace retirement account or not, I suggest opening a Roth IRA (if your income level is below a specified limit). The benefits of a Roth are unique and span generations.

Although contributions into the account are made with after tax dollars, the money in the account grows tax free and may be withdrawn in retirement tax free as well. You may begin withdrawing your contributions at age 59 ½ (or earlier under certain circumstances) but are also welcome to leave the money (tax free) to your heirs.

In general, the more you invest into tax advantaged accounts, and the earlier you begin, the more your wealth will grow.

Juan's Investing Story

Here's the proof for this investing approach.

When you implement these simple steps you will create an investment portfolio which beats the professionals and leads to a large sum of money for your future. Take a look at Juan and Jenna's stories to motivate you to start investing today.

At age 25, Juan started contributing $350 per month into his retirement account. He automatically transferred the money from his paycheck into the account. He decided to invest 25 percent in a bond index fund and 75 percent into an all world stock index fund.

Assume 7 percent average annual investment returns.

Juan's employer kicked in an additional $175 per month, for a total monthly retirement fund contribution of $525. Each year, Juan invested $6,300 for retirement; $4,200 payroll deduction along with the employer's $2,100 matching contribution.

After setting up the transfer and choosing the funds, he didn't think much about it.

After a small input into savings for emergencies and short-term goals, Juan spent the rest of his paycheck, knowing his financial future was secure.

Over 40 years, when Juan reached the age of 65, his $168,000 investment plus the employer's $84,000 (total contribution of $252,000) grew to over $1,386,065.

Juan never increased his retirement contributions!

Imagine if Juan had increased his contributions as his income grew. **With compounding returns, your original investment makes money on top of money.**

Look at the retirement contributions in a different way.

Juan invests $4,200 each year. That's 10 percent of a $42,000 income. Yet, $4,200 per year is only 7 percent of a $60,000 salary. As Juan's salary increases, he can contribute a smaller percent of his income and still reach over a million dollars by retirement, or, as his salary increases, he can choose to increase his retirement contributions.

The key to building a large nest egg for the future is to start investing younger, to give your money more time to compound.

TRANSFER MONEY INTO THE ACCOUNT AS SOON AS IT'S OPENED

Follow human resources procedure to transfer a specific amount from your paycheck into either your workplace retirement account or investment brokerage account.

The automatic transfer ensures that every pay period money goes into the investment account.

More questions? Ask your bank or investment broker for help.

Still not convinced that starting earlier is better?

Jenna's Investing Story

Jenna didn't start saving for retirement until she was 40. Let's see how much Jenna has for retirement at age 65.

To keep things simple, we'll use the exact same monthly contributions as Juan. The only difference is that Jenna starts investing 15 years after Juan.

Jenna invests $350 per month and her employer kicks in another $175 per month for a total of $525 per month, or $6,300 retirement investing per year. Assume Jenna's investments also earn a 7 percent return in stock and bond mutual funds.

Just like Juan, Jenna stops investing at age 65.

The results of Jenna's late start are a significantly lower retirement nest egg for Jenna.

Over 25 years, when Jenna reached age 65, her $105,000 investment plus the employer's $52,500 (total contribution of $157,500) grew to over $427,768.

Jenna and her employer invested a total of $157,000 and she had $427,768 upon retirement.

Juan and his employer invested a total of $252,000 and he had a retirement account worth $1,386,065 at age 65, Juan started earlier, invested for 40 years, and his retirement account investments compounded over five times.

Jenna started later and her account increased almost three times over the 25 years she invested.

Juan and Jennas' Retirement Savings					
Juan starts investing for retirement at age 25. Jenna starts investing for retirement at age 40. Both retire at age 65.					
	Juan & Jennas' monthly contribution	Employers' monthly contribution	Average annual return	Total contributed (includes employers' contribution)	Amount available at age 65
Juan	$350	$175	7.00%	$252,000	$1,386,065
Jenna	$359	$175	7.00%	$157,500	$427,768

This isn't to say that $427,768 is lousy retirement account value. **In fact, it's great to know that late starters still have a chance to build up a retirement fund.**

Let's not ignore the fact that Juan did contribute more money than Jenna, and so we wouldn't expect Jenna to have as much money at retirement. But it's tough to ignore that

Juan (and his employer's contribution) increased five and a half times, whereas Jenna and her employer's total investment grew 2.7 times.

Imagine if you late starters contribute a bit more than $525 (combined employer and employee) per month into a retirement account. As you'd assume, a greater monthly contribution will yield a larger retirement nest egg.

START INVESTING TODAY

Start investing for retirement today, no matter how old you are. And even if you're age 40 or older, try to find a few more dollars a month to start putting toward retirement.

Realize that even the smallest amount of money can compound and grow over time. Starting to save and invest today is better than putting your future on hold.

SUMMARY

✓ Set up automatic transfer into a retirement account now.

✓ Time in the markets is a great predictor of long-term wealth.

✓ Contribute more than you think you can afford.

✓ If you haven't started saving for retirement yet, start investing today, no matter how old you are.

Chapter 8:
Target Date Funds-
Pros and Cons

"Planning is bringing the future into the present so that you can do something about it now."

Alan Lakein

WHAT IS A TARGET DATE FUND?

Are you interested in buying one fund which holds all the stock and bond investments you need? A target date fund can be compared with a big box retailer or a shopping mall. In the shopping mall, you can buy everything you need at one site. In a target date fund, you get all of your investing needs met with one fund.

Here's how it works.

A company, such as Vanguard, Fidelity or countless others, create a mutual fund for investors expecting to retire in a specific year. The premise is that the fund offers diverse financial assets including stock and bond mutual funds in one 'fund of funds'. If you are thinking about retiring in 2040, then you would invest in the target date fund 2040.

With many years until the target or retirement date, the money is initially invested more aggressively. As the target (or retirement) date approaches, the asset mix shifts to a more conservative allocation.

This asset mix chart includes Fidelity, T. Rowe Price, and Vanguard asset allocations for each target date fund. You'll notice that the asset mix percentages vary among the three firms.

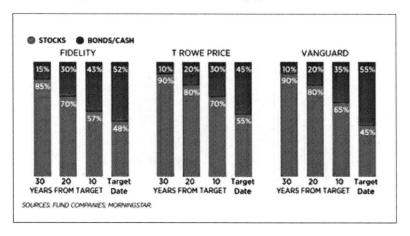

Take a look at the Fidelity Target date fund. With 30 years until retirement, this fund has an asset allocation of 85 percent stock mutual funds and 15 percent fixed or bond type mutual funds. As time progresses and the fund moves towards its target date, the asset mix becomes more conservative with greater percentages allocated to bonds and lesser percentages invested in stock assets. A 30-year-old in 2015 who wants to retire at age 65 would buy the 2015 plus 35 or 2050 target date fund.

Notice that T. Rowe Price and Vanguards' target date funds choose different asset allocations during their lives. For example, with ten years until retirement, Fidelity has 57% stock investments and 43% fixed. At the same juncture, Vanguard is more aggressive with 65% stocks and the balance in bonds. Finally, T.Rowe price is the most aggressive. With ten years until retirement, the T.Rowe price target date fund still holds 70 percent in the risky stock asset class. That may be too aggressive for the moderate 55 year old investor.

Before you commit to what appears to be the 'perfect' investment solution, consider that, as with any investment, there are advantages and disadvantages to a target date fund.

TARGET DATE FUND ADVANTAGES

It doesn't get any easier than this. A target date fund takes almost all of the work out of investing. Once you decide on the fund target year, all you do is transfer your money in. The fund invests the contribution and rebalances according to the mandates of that particular target date fund. You can see from the previous sample asset allocation graphs that each target date fund is rebalanced periodically to reflect an asset allocation which starts out more aggressively and becomes more conservative over time.

For the simplest investing approach, you could purchase a target date fund for a particular retirement date, or another future date. Parents may consider a target date fund to align with the date Junior starts college.

Many workplace retirement accounts offer target date funds, making it easy to choose one with the appropriate date. If you select this option in your workplace retirement account, then every pay period your contributions are transferred into the fund. If you have another retirement account outside work, such as an IRA or Roth IRA, you can purchase a target date fund in that discount brokerage account as well.

This may sound like the perfect investment approach, and for some it is. If you prefer not to do any investment oversight at all, a target date fund may be for you—or maybe not.

TARGET DATE FUND DISADVANTAGES

Target date funds have cons as well as pros.

You've learned the importance of keeping fees low when investing. When a company is bundling several mutual funds under one umbrella, you may end up paying two layers of fees. And those expenses add up over time.

According to Forbes' Tom Anderson in "Should You Trust Your Retirement To A Target Date Fund?"[1] Vanguard is the only company whose target date funds consist solely of low cost index funds.

The Vanguard Investment Company reports expense ratios significantly below the industry average. "Vanguard Target Retirement Funds"[2] average expense ratios are a meager 0.17 percent. Industry average expense ratio for comparable target-date funds are almost six times higher at 1.05 percent according to Vanguard and Lipper, as of December 31, 2013.

If you're paying 1 percent more in fees year in and year out, then that's a percent that is not invested and compounding your wealth.

The asset allocation is another potential problem.

As you learned in "Chapter 4: Are You a Risk Taker or Risk Avoider?" your risk tolerance and risk capacity varies. If you are a conservative investor who suffers anxiety at the smallest decline in your investment portfolio, then you may be unhappy at age 40 with 80 percent of your portfolio in stock mutual funds. At that allocation, a 25 percent drop in the stock market will cause a 20 percent decline in your total investment portfolio (assuming the bond returns remain constant).

So if your total retirement account is worth $10,000, the 20 decline leaves you with $8,000. A drop like that, for a conservative investor, may cause extreme discomfort and a tendency to sell. And it's helpful to understand that selling 'low' is rarely a good idea.

For the investor who's risk picture doesn't fit in with the target date funds, this investment may cause greater stress than constructing her own portfolio.

According to Ted Haagen of Ted Haagen Financial Group, as reported by Bankrate's Jennifer Lawler in "Target-date Fund Pros and Cons"[3], target date funds may only rebalance every few years. This infrequent rebalancing can cost the fund in lost returns. Annual rebalancing is likely to increase returns while keeping risk levels in control.

Target date funds are not risk free, nor do they offer a guaranteed return. Although this type of investment simplifies the oversight and management of your money, its returns go up and down just like those of any stock or bond investment.

Rose and Dylan's Target Date Funds

Rose is 35 years of age in 2015. She expects to retire in 30 years at age 65, in the year 2045.

If she chooses the 2045 fund from Vanguard, then the current asset allocation is approximately 90 percent stocks, 10 percent fixed investments. By retirement, this 2045 target date fund's asset allocation would hold 50 percent stock investments and 50 percent fixed investments.

Notice that the current 90 percent stock allocation is very aggressive and, if the stock market experiences a large decline, so will Rose's fund assets. If Rose is a moderately conservative investor, and experiences a 20 percent decline in her retirement assets one year, she may be extremely unhappy and be tempted to sell.

Dylan is also 35 in 2015. He also expects to retire in 30 years at the age of 65, in the year 2045.

If he chooses the Fidelity Target Date fund, then his retirement asset allocation looks like this initially; 85 percent stock assets and 15 percent bond investments. This allocation is more conservative than Vanguard's. After 30 years, at the target date, this Fidelity fund continues to be invested more conservatively. Upon retirement, the stock assets in the Fidelity fund equal 48 percent and the bonds and cash or fixed portion of the portfolio is 52 percent.

As Rose and Dylans' choices demonstrate, you can't blindly invest in a target date fund and go to sleep for the next 30 years. You should consider your risk profile, the fund's fees, the fund's asset allocation and how all these factors fit together.

First review the target date fund; next consider your own situation and risk profile. Only then can you decide whether a target date fund is the right choice for you or not.

SUMMARY

✓ A target date fund is designed for individuals who want to invest in one diversified fund throughout their entire working life, and leave the rebalancing and fund selection to the manager of the target date fund.

✓ An advantage of a target date fund is that, after selecting a fund, you have no additional oversight.

✓ Several problems with the target date fund include higher fees and the possibility that the percentages allocated to stocks and bonds may be too aggressive for your risk level.

Chapter 9:
Final Tips and Rebalancing Guide for a Portfolio That Beats Active Fund Managers

"The individual investor should act consistently as an investor and not as a speculator."

Ben Graham

CREATE AND MANAGE A SUCCESSFUL INVESTMENT PORTFOLIO

You've got the basics of a winning investment portfolio. But there are a few more concepts to understand before you're finished. This chapter ties up some loose ends.

You'll learn the difference between an investment and an account (and why knowing what distinguishes the two is important).

You'll find out a bit more about risk in investing and get an introduction into a worst case scenario. Finally, the rebalancing section will give you a tool to simply and quickly manage your investments.

What's the difference Between the Basket and the Fruit?

This pet peeve of mine is going to be cleared up right here. When I ask someone what type of investments they hold, they frequently respond, "I have a 401(k)." Someone once responded, "I have a Roth IRA at Schwab."

What's wrong with that response? Does that sound like a perfectly appropriate response to you? Please, humor me for a minute.

Consider a basket, filled with fruit.

An account is like the basket. The fruit in the basket is akin to the individual funds, bonds, stocks, and other financial assets.

An investment is an individual stock, like Apple (AAPL) stock, or an index mutual fund, such as the Vanguard Total Market Index Fund (VTSMX).

So, when you're asked what type of investments you hold, consider the name of the funds or individual stocks. You might respond, "I have an international index fund, a diversified bond fund, and a U.S. stock index fund."

Why does this matter?

The whole gist of investing to beat active fund managers' results goes back to creating an investment portfolio with index funds. In order to do this, it's helpful to understand the difference between an investment and an account.

LOOK AT THE WHOLE PIE—UNDERSTAND YOUR ASSET ALLOCATION

This section shows you how to efficiently manage your investment accounts.

Many of you have more than one investment account. You may have a 401(k) at work, a discount investment brokerage account at TD Ameritrade, a certificate of deposit at a bank, and others.

It's key to examine all of your investment accounts together, when creating your asset allocation.

Let's take a look at Jamal's situation.

Jamal works at Greentree Enterprises where he has a 401(k) retirement account worth $30,000. In his account, he has $10,000 in T. Rowe Price Total Equity Market Index Fund (POMIX), $10,000 in T. Rowe Price International Equity Index Fund (PIEQX), and $10,000 in T. Rowe Price Inflation Protected Bond Fund.

So far, Jamal's portfolio looks quite simple:

33.4% U.S. Stock Fund

33.3% International Stock Fund

33.3% Inflation Protected Bond Index Fund

If those were Jamal's only investments, his asset allocation would be 66.7 percent stock assets and 33.3 percent bond assets.

But wait, Jamal has other investments outside of his 401(k). He has a Treasury Direct Account with $10,000 of Government I Bonds. He also has an investment account at Fidelity with $5,000 in a small cap U.S. Index Fund and $5,000 in an International Bond Fund.

Now it's not so easy to see his asset allocation.

In order to figure out Jamal's asset allocation pie, imagine that all of his investments are in one basket. Next, figure out what percent of the total basket goes into each asset class.

Jamal's Asset Allocation

Stock Assets

For this example, we ignore the accounts and simply look at the individual mutual funds.

$10,000 – T.Rowe Price U.S. Stock index fund
$10,000 – T.Rowe Price International Stock Index Fund
<u>$5,000 – Small Cap U.S. Index Fund</u>
$25,000-Stock Assets

Fixed Assets

$5,000 - International Bond Fund
$10,000 - Government I Bonds
<u>$10,000 - T. Rowe Price Inflation Protected Bond Fund</u>
$25,000-Fixed Bond Assets

Total Value of Jamal's Investment Portfolio

$50,000

To sum up Jamal's portfolio, first we need to break it down. He has three distinct investment accounts; one at TreasuryDirect.com (I bonds), another at his workplace 401(k), which offers T.Rowe Price funds, and a third discount investment brokerage account at Fidelity Investments. Each of these accounts hold different investments.

WHAT IS JAMAL'S ASSET ALLOCATION?

He has $25,000 in stock assets and $25,000 in fixed assets. His asset allocation is 50% ($25,000/$50,000) in stock assets and 50% in fixed assets, a very conservative asset allocation.

Jamal is only 35 years old, with a steady job and a moderate risk tolerance. He didn't even realize that he had such a conservative asset allocation.

Not only is Jamal's asset allocation quite conservative, his U.S. bond allocation lacks any exposure to the higher yielding corporate bond sector and only includes government bonds.

Do you think this is the right asset allocation for Jamal? Probably not.

Jamal decides to rebalance and align his portfolio with his age and moderate risk tolerance. He decides to apportion a higher percent to stock investments and a lower percent in bond investments. He should probably shoot for 60 or 65 percent in stock assets and the rest in the fixed class. These adjustments are more consistent with Jamal's age and risk comfort level.

SUCCESSFUL PORTFOLIO MANAGEMENT-REBALANCE TO BOOST RETURNS

Rebalancing means selling, buying, and/or investing new monies in your investment portfolio in a way to get the percentage allocations in line with your initial preferred allocation.

For example, assume your preferred asset allocation mix is 50% stock; 50% fixed. At the end of the year, after a run up in the stock market assume your asset allocation looks like this: 60% stocks and 40% fixed assets.

You are best off 'rebalancing' to return to your desired fifty-fifty asset allocation.

Why Rebalance?

There are reams of research recommending rebalancing your investment portfolio. The advantages include buying low and selling high along with boosting long-term returns. Although there are a variety of opinions regarding how often to rebalance, once a year is enough to gain the rebalancing benefits.

In Jamal's example we touched on the rebalancing activity. Next, you'll get another crack at the mechanics of this important portfolio management task.

How Does Rebalancing Work?

Marina's desired asset allocation is 65% stock investments and 35% fixed investments.

Marina holds 65% of her investment portfolio in an all world stock index fund. The remaining 35% of her investment portfolio is in a diversified U.S. Bond Index mutual fund. She makes monthly contributions into her retirement account, in line with her 65% stock versus 35% fixed proportions.

On December 31st, her investment portfolio is worth $100,000. She calculates her asset allocation by dividing the stock portion of her investments by $100,000 and doing the same for the fixed portion.

Here's her asset allocation on December 31st, after a robust year of excellent stock market returns: $70,000 in an all world stock index fund and $30,000 in the U.S. bond fund.

Instead of her desired 65% stock versus 35% fixed asset allocation, her stock investments grew more than the bonds and, thus, on December 31st, her asset allocation was 70% stocks (70,000/100,000) versus 30% bonds (30,000/100,000).

In order to get back to her original 65% stock; 35% bond allocation, she has several choices. She can immediately sell $5,000—or 5% of the stock investments—and use the proceeds to buy $5,000 or 5% of bond investment.

Another, more gradual approach is to change her future investments and contribute more to the bond index fund and less to the all-world stock fund and let the asset allocation return to the preferred mix over time.

Marina could contribute 60% to stocks and 40% to bonds and check the asset allocation again in six months to see if she's closer to her preferred 65% stock versus 35% bond mix.

Rebalancing doesn't need to be an exact science. Since financial asset prices change every day, it's impossible to keep a perfectly allocated portfolio unless you buy and sell every day, which is not recommended.

The beauty of this investment approach is its simplicity.

Thus, you don't want to make it more complex by trying to keep your portfolio asset allocation 'perfect'.

Less management and oversight is usually better. Simply input your portfolio values and changes every quarter and rebalance every year. And do not look at your investment values every day. Expect that they will vary and have confidence in the strength of the overall world markets.

REDUCE TAXES BY MODIFYING YOUR ASSET ALLOCATION

Certain accounts in which you place various types of assets can increase your total returns. Why? Because stock dividends, bond dividends, and asset capital gains and losses all have distinct tax treatments. Another way to beat active fund managers' returns is to pay less tax.

Although tax law is fluid, in general, capital gains and dividends are taxed at a lower rate than interest or ordinary income. Interest income is usually taxed at a higher rate.

It makes sense to place the highest taxed investments in tax protected retirement accounts where you can defer tax payments. (Jamal couldn't place all of his bond investments into the tax favored retirement account because a diversified corporate bond index fund wasn't available in his employer's plan.)

Most equity investments have capital gains and dividends, which are taxed at a lower rate. Place more of these type of stock mutual funds in a taxable discount brokerage account if possible.

Bonds, REITs and other fixed income investments that generate regular interest payments are presently taxed as ordinary income, which may be higher than the capital gains rates. Due to the annual tax bill for these investments, they're better suited for placement in your retirement accounts, 401(k) and IRA (Roth and Traditional), whenever possible.

HOPE FOR THE BEST; EXPECT THE WORST—BEST AND WORST STOCK MARKET RETURNS

Education and information can keep you from buying high and selling low. In other words, understanding historical asset prices can keep you from doing something stupid that will compromise your long-term wealth.

This section presents some past 'worst case scenarios' in an attempt to keep you from panic when the next market downturn arrives.

According to Dana Anspach in an *About Money; Money Over 55.com* article, "Best and Worst Rolling Index Returns 1973-Mid 2009" [1], over the short run, there's tremendous variability in stock market returns. Over the long-term, the risk is much lower.

Remember, when looking at these examples, we're only looking at stock market returns. Most of you will have a portfolio of stocks and fixed assets. Thus, even if your stock investments drop 15 percent, due to a percent of your assets in bonds, your total investment portfolio value will fall much less (as long as bond returns hold steady).

Let's check out some best and worst case scenarios.

First, the short-term perspective.

The worst one year stock performance between 1973 and 2009 is relatively recent with a -43 percent return for the year ending February, 2009.

In contrast, the 61 percent best one year stock market return during the last 40 years happened over the twelve months ending in June of 1983. That's over a 100 percent difference between best and worst.

The best two decade average return was 18 percent per year over the twenty year period ending in March, 2000.

Now for a long-term worst case scenario.

From 1973 through mid-2009, the worst twenty year return for the U.S. stock market was 7 percent per year. The worst 20 year time period in recent record ended in February, 2009. Even during the worst time period in recent history, if you kept your money invested, didn't try to time the market by jumping in and out, the stock portion of your investments from March, 1989 through February, 2009 gained a respectable 7 percent annually.

To sum it up, the worst case scenario during the short-term is quite scary, but if you have the fortitude and confidence in the U.S. and world markets to stay invested through the ups and downs, you're likely to experience investment results that will beat the professional active mutual fund managers.

THIS IS HOW INDEX FUND INVESTING IN LINE WITH YOUR ASSET ALLOCATION BEATS THE PROS

Add up the benefit of index fund investing, keeping management costs rock bottom, minimizing taxes, and rebalancing each year, and your portfolio is likely to beat that of actively managed investment portfolios.

In very little time, you've created and are managing a successful investment portfolio. The result of this index fund investing approach is to outperform the pros as well as grow your dollars enough to supplement your Social Security payments and give you enough money for a satisfying retirement.

Isn't that the point of investing? Spread your earnings out over your entire life so you enjoy a wealthy life now and later.

SUMMARY

✓ An investment account is different from an individual investment. The account is similar to a basket and the individual fund or investment is like the fruit contained within the basket.

✓ View all assets, regardless of the account, as a whole, in order to figure out your asset allocation.

✓ Locate assets to minimize taxes. Keep taxable bonds in tax protected retirement accounts and index stock funds in taxable investment accounts whenever possible.

✓ Understand market risk and return by looking at best and worst case scenarios. You'll be a more successful investor if you avoid market timing.

✓ Each year, rebalance back to your preferred allocation the proportion invested in stocks and fixed assets.

END NOTES

This book is written to strip off the investing pitches and hyperbole.

Put into practice these tenets and spend less time managing your money and more time living your life. That way, once you set up your investment portfolio, if you don't want to read any more about investing, you don't need to.

If you'd like a list of recommended investing books, stop by the Barbara Friedberg Personal Finance.com Wealth Shop (http://barbarafriedbergpersonalfinance.com/wealth-shop/).

For more investing information visit Barbara Friedberg Personal Finance (http://barbarafriedbergpersonalfinance.com/). I welcome your comments and questions.

I offer a free Wealth Tips Newsletter (http://barbarafriedbergpersonalfinance.com/investing-rules-wealth-tips) filled with money solutions for saving, investing and personal finance.

To contact me directly, please visit my personal contact page (http://barbarafriedbergpersonalfinance.com/contact/)

Caveat: This book is for information purposes only and not a recommendation to buy or sell any particular financial assets. I may receive a commission to cover expenses if you invest in a product mentioned in this book.

NOTES

CHAPTER 1: WHAT IS THE INVESTING STRATEGY THAT BEATS THE PROS?

1. Philips, Christopher B., Francis M. Kinniry Fr., Todd Schlanger, & Joshua M. Hirt. 2014. "The Case for Index-Fund Investing". *Vanguard*. Retrieved from https://pressroom.vanguard.com/content/nonindex ed/Updated_The_Case_for_Index_Fund_Investing _4.9.2014.pdf.

2. Friedberg, Barbara. 2013. "I Bonds Demystified; Get Good Returns On Your Cash". *Barbara Friedberg Personal Finance.com*. http://barbarafriedbergpersonalfinance.com/i-bonds-demystified-best-cash-investment/

3. Damodoran, Answar. 2014. "Annual Returns of Stock, T. Bonds and T. Bills: 1928-Current". Retrieved from http://pages.stern.nyu.edu/~adamodar/New_Home _Page/datafile/histretSP.html.

CHAPTER 2: BE SMART - BEFORE YOU INVEST SET THE STAGE FOR INVESTING SUCCESS

1. Friedberg, Barbara. 2013. "I Bonds Demystified; Get Good Returns On Your Cash". *Barbara Friedberg Personal Finance.com*.

http://barbarafriedbergpersonalfinance.com/i-bonds-demystified-best-cash-investment/

2. Friedberg, Barbara. "What Does Price Earnings (PE) Ratio Mean?" *Barbara Friedberg Personal Finance.com*. Date accessed, October 24, 2014. http://barbarafriedbergpersonalfinance.com/does-price-earnings-pe-ratio-mean/

CHAPTER 3: DO YOU NEED AN ADVISOR?

1. Moyer, Liz. August 9, 2014. "Taking Stock of Automated Advisers." *The Wall Street Journal*. p. b7.

CHAPTER 5: WHICH INVESTMENTS GO IN YOUR INVESTMENT PORTFOLIO?

1. Investment Company Institute. 2014. "2014 Investment Company Fact Book, 54th edition." Accessed October 24, 2014. http://www.icifactbook.org/pdf/14_fb_table01.pdf.

2. Prior, Anna. 2013. "Build a Portfolio That's as Simple as One, Two, Three". *The Wall Street Journal*. July 7. http://online.wsj.com/articles/SB10001424127887323566804578551793835572924

3. Morningstar Website. 2014. Accessed October 25, 2014. http://www.morningstar.com/

CHAPTER 6: BLUEPRINT FOR AN INDEX FUND PORTFOLIO (FOR YOUR RISK LEVEL) THAT BEATS THE PROS

1. Friedberg, Barbara. "I Bonds Demystified; Get Good Returns On Your Cash". *Barbara Friedberg Personal Finance.com*. Date accessed, October 26, 2014. http://barbarafriedbergpersonalfinance.com/i-bonds-demystified-best-cash-investment/

2. Friedberg, Barbara. "Investing Lazy Portfolios Drill Down". *Barbara Friedberg Personal Finance.com*. Date accessed October 26, 2014. http://barbarafriedbergpersonalfinance.com/investing-lazy-portfolios-farrell-marketwatch/

CHAPTER 7: QUICK START GUIDE FOR A 6-7 FIGURE RETIREMENT ACCOUNT

1. Friedberg, Barbara. 2014. "Fidelity's Retirement Savings Guidelines". *Barbara Friedberg Personal Finance.com*. Date accessed October 26, 2014. http://barbarafriedbergpersonalfinance.com/fidelitys-retirement-savings-guidelines/

2. Friedberg, Barbara. 2011. "Reader Question; Roth or 401 K, Which to Max Out First?" *Barbara Friedberg Personal Finance.com*. Date accessed October 26, 2014. http://barbarafriedbergpersonalfinance.com/reader-question-roth-or-k-which-max-out-first/

3. Friedberg, Barbara. 2013. "SEP IRA or Solo 401(k) - Which is Better?" *Barbara Friedberg Personal Finance.com*. Date accessed October 26, 2014. http://barbarafriedbergpersonalfinance.com/sep-ira-versus-solo-401k-which-better/

CHAPTER 8: TARGET DATE FUNDS - PROS AND CONS

1. Anderson, Tom. 2012. "Should You Trust your Retirement to a Target Date Fund?" *Forbes.com*. Date accessed October 28, 2014. http://www.forbes.com/sites/janetnovack/2012/06/06/should-you-trust-your-retirement-to-a-target-date-fund/

2. Vanguard. 2014. "Vanguard Target Retirement Funds". Date accessed October 28, 2014. https://investor.vanguard.com/mutual-funds/target-retirement/#/

3. Lawler, Jennifer. 2014. "Target-date Fund Pros and Cons". *Bankrate.com*. Date accessed, October 28, 2014. http://www.bankrate.com/finance/retirement/target-date-fund-pros-and-cons-1.aspx.

CHAPTER 9: FINAL TIPS AND REBALANCING GUIDE FOR A PORTFOLIO THAT BEATS ACTIVE FUND MANAGERS

1. Anspach, Dana. 2009. "Best and Worst Rolling Index Returns 1973-Mid 2009". *About Money.com*. Date accessed, October 29, 2014.

http://moneyover55.about.com/od/stockmarketretu
rns/ig/Stock-Market-
Performance/sp500_index_rolling_returns.htm

FREE BONUS DOWNLOAD

Complimentary Micro book, Barbara Friedberg Personal Finance; The Readers' Favorites
http://forms.aweber.com/form/43/1333323943.htm

Please enjoy this complimentary micro book as my gift to you.

This specially crafted micro book includes 35 pages of Barbara Friedberg Personal Finance.com Readers' Favorites articles. There is something here for everyone.

AMAZON REVIEW

If you benefited from this book, please leave an Amazon review. This helps other readers learn to *Invest and Beat the Pros; How to Create and Manage a Successful Investment Portfolio.*

OTHER BOOKS BY BARBARA FRIEDBERG

How to Get Rich; Without Winning the Lottery
http://barbarafriedbergpersonalfinance.com/How to Get Rich

Personal Finance: An Encyclopedia of
Modern Money Management
http://barbarafriedbergpersonalfinance.com/Personal Finance Encyclopedia

WHAT OTHERS ARE SAYING ABOUT BARBARA FRIEDBERG'S INVESTING EXPERTISE.

"I'm excited to see that many of your articles are showing up in the top 25 most viewed posts. It means that people may be coming back to the site itself on a regular basis to look at your work, which is good news.

Thanks for providing an easy but detailed step-by-step guide for the average investor."

-Casey Quinlan,
U.S. News and World Report

"Barbara focuses on first encouraging you to understand your own style. She tackles risk tolerance, and provides you with different scenarios, depending on your ability to handle risk. As with so many things in life, one of the keys to success with investing is understanding yourself.

Her portfolio advice is simple and effective. She places emphasis on taking the first step right now, and then building on it as you go.

In a world where low-cost index funds make it possible for you to invest with an acceptable level of risk management, and without the need for an understanding of P/E ratios, there really isn't a reason why you can't set things up right now.

Barbara places a great deal of emphasis on asset allocation, which is a good way to go. You can use the sample portfolios illustrated by Friedberg to choose index funds that make sense for your individual situation.

Barbara writes clearly and concisely. When you read this investing book, you will understand what you need to do, and have a clear method of putting your plan into action."

- **Miranda Marquit,**
Financial expert, freelance journalist,
and PlantingMoneySeeds.com editor

"I feel so much more informed after reading your work. Portfolio assets have been a conundrum to me while I consider how to take the leap forward with my finances. You managed to simplify it and provide insight on whether bonds are currently a good investment.

Barb, you are a financial magician!"

-**Ronnie,**
All the Frugal Ladies.com

"I love this Risk Quiz from Barbara Friedberg's Invest and Beat the Pros. I will be sharing it from client social media accounts this afternoon."

Sleep at Night Guide to Risk© (included in Invest and Beat the Pros - Create & Manage a Successful Investment Portfolio) comment.

-**Linsey Knerl,**
KnerlFamilyMedia.com owner
and personal finance expert

Made in the USA
San Bernardino, CA
02 January 2016